I0814861

DISCOVERING THE UNITED STATES

New Jersey

BY JANET SLINGERLAND

Kids Core
An Imprint of Abdo Publishing
abdobooks.com

abdobooks.com

Published by Abdo Publishing, a division of ABDO, PO Box 398166, Minneapolis, Minnesota 55439.

Printed in China.
052024
092024

THIS BOOK CONTAINS RECYCLED MATERIALS

Cover Photo: Stefan Tomic/iStockphoto
Interior Photos: Bettmann/Getty Images, 4–5; E. Q. Roy/Shutterstock Images, 6; Shutterstock Images, 7, 9 (bottom left), 12–13, 20–21, 22, 28 (Ocean City); Danita Delimont/Shutterstock Images, 9 (top left); Cinema Photo/Shutterstock Images, 9 (top right); Jay Ondreicka/Shutterstock Images, 9 (bottom right); Bruce Goerlitz Photo/Shutterstock Images, 10; Kena Betancur/AFP/Getty Images, 14; Ezume Images/Shutterstock Images, 16; iStockphoto, 18; Jon Bilous/Shutterstock Images, 24, 28 (Delaware Water Gap); Dennis MacDonald/Shutterstock Images, 25; Daniel Petty/Denver Post/Getty Images, 26; Red Line Editorial, 28 (map), 29

Editor: Haley Williams
Series Designer: Katharine Hale

Library of Congress Control Number: 2023949359

Publisher's Cataloging-in-Publication Data

Names: Slingerland, Janet, author.
Title: New Jersey / by Janet Slingerland
Description: Minneapolis, Minnesota: Abdo Publishing, 2025 | Series: Discovering the United States | Includes online resources and index.
Identifiers: ISBN 9781098294007 (lib. bdg.) | ISBN 9798384913276 (ebook)
Subjects: LCSH: U.S. states--Juvenile literature. | New Jersey--History--Juvenile literature. | Northeastern States--Juvenile literature. | Physical geography--United States--Juvenile literature.
Classification: DDC 973--dc23

All population data taken from:
"Estimates of Population by Sex, Race, and Hispanic Origin: April 1, 2020 to July 1, 2022." *US Census Bureau, Population Division*, June 2023, census.gov.

CONTENTS

Aaron Burr, *left,* thought the insults of Alexander Hamilton, *right*, had stopped Burr from becoming the governor of New York. That led to their famous duel.

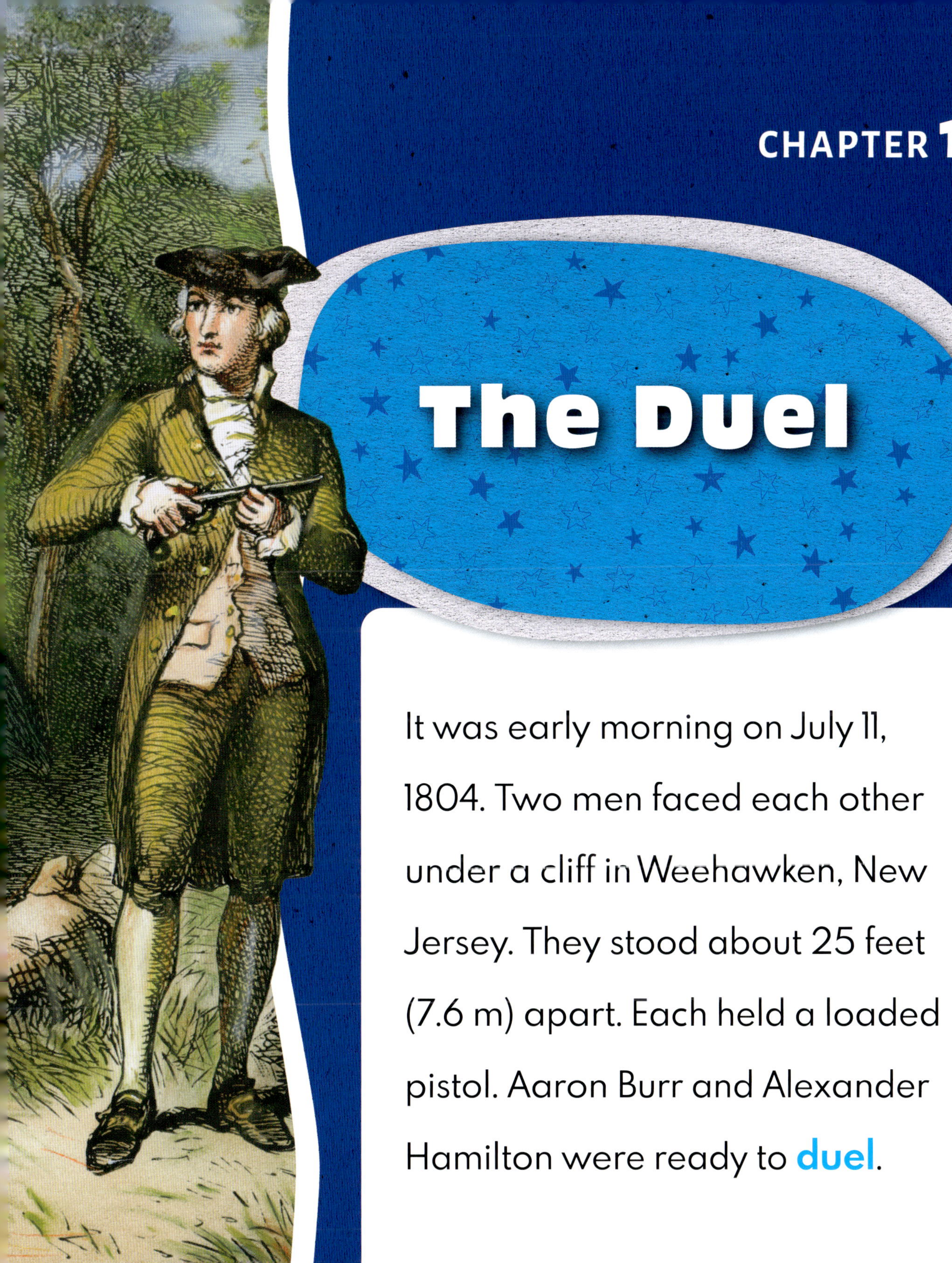

CHAPTER 1

The Duel

It was early morning on July 11, 1804. Two men faced each other under a cliff in Weehawken, New Jersey. They stood about 25 feet (7.6 m) apart. Each held a loaded pistol. Aaron Burr and Alexander Hamilton were ready to **duel**.

Today, people can visit the Weehawken Dueling Grounds and see where Hamilton and Burr dueled.

Burr and Hamilton were famous American politicians. Burr was vice president. Hamilton was the former secretary of the treasury. They were **rivals** for years. In 1804, Burr believed Hamilton had insulted him. So he challenged Hamilton to a duel.

After a count of ten, the men raised their pistols and fired. Hamilton shot a tree. Burr hit Hamilton in the stomach. Hamilton died. Burr wasn't charged with murder. He also never

Beach towns like Ocean City are popular summer spots in New Jersey.

faced a trial. But his political career was ruined. Today, Hamilton and Burr's duel in New Jersey remains a notable moment in early US history.

New Jersey's Land

New Jersey is in the US region called the Northeast. Pennsylvania borders the state to the west. New York is to the north. The Atlantic Ocean makes up most of the state's eastern border. Delaware Bay lies to the south. And the Delaware River flows along the western border.

The land in New Jersey is different throughout the state. Northwestern New Jersey is covered by hills and mountains. This area of

Water, Water Everywhere

New Jersey is bordered by water on three sides. All but about 50 miles (80 km) of the state's boundary touches water. New Jersey also has 6,450 miles (10,380 km) of rivers. There are more than 11,000 ponds and lakes as well.

New Jersey Facts

DATE OF STATEHOOD
December 18, 1787

CAPITAL
Trenton

POPULATION
9,261,699

AREA
8,723 square miles
(22,592 sq km)

STATE BIRD

Eastern goldfinch

STATE TREE

Northern red oak

STATE FLOWER

Violet

STATE REPTILE

Bog turtle

Each US state has a different population, size, and capital city. States also have state symbols.

the state is rocky and wooded. Moving south and east, the land gets flatter and wetter. Central and southern New Jersey have forests and swamps. There are sandy beaches along the coast.

The tallest mountain in New Jersey is called High Point. From the top, visitors can see into both New York and Pennsylvania.

Many different plants and animals can be found in New Jersey. This includes more than 700 endangered species. Birds such as bald eagles and piping plovers nest in the state. Tiny bog turtles live in the wetlands. A plant known as seabeach amaranth grows along the coastline.

New Jersey's Climate

New Jersey experiences four seasons. The mountains are cooler than the rest of the state.

In the winter, the northwest tends to get the most snow. The weather is milder near the coast. There is less snow there in the winter. In the summer, ocean breezes keep the coast cooler.

New Jersey gets rain or snow about 120 days each year. About 45 inches (114 cm) of precipitation falls during that time. The driest months are in the fall.

Further Evidence

Look at the website below. Does it give any new evidence to support Chapter One?

New Jersey

abdocorelibrary.com/discovering-new-jersey

New Jersey's state flag was adopted in 1896.

CHAPTER 2

The People of New Jersey

The first people in New Jersey lived there starting about 10,000 years ago. They are known as the Lenni-Lenape. These American Indians hunted and fished. They also grew crops such as squash and corn. Today, three tribes are recognized by New Jersey.

The BAPS Swaminarayan Akshardham temple in Robbinsdale, New Jersey, is the largest Hindu temple located outside of India.

They are the Nanticoke Lenni-Lenape, Powhatan Renape, and Ramapough Lenape.

In the early 1660s, Dutch, Swedish, and Finnish people **settled** in New Jersey. Then in 1664, the British took control of the state.

It became one of the original 13 **colonies**. During the early 1900s, more Europeans moved to New Jersey. This included people from Germany and Ireland.

In 2022, just under 9.3 million people lived in New Jersey. White people made up about 53 percent of the population. About 22 percent were Hispanic or Latino. Black people made up 15 percent. About 11 percent of people were Asian.

Culture

New Jersey has many food traditions. One of the most unique is pork roll. It was created in Trenton in 1856. Pork is mixed with spices. It is then rolled into a log and smoked.

Pork roll is also known as Taylor Ham. It was named after the creator, John Taylor.

New Jerseyans have a favorite way to eat pork roll. They slice and fry it. Then they put it on an egg-and-cheese sandwich.

The Devils hockey team is New Jersey's only major professional sports team. But several New York teams also play home games in the state. This includes the New York Jets and New York Giants football teams. Many New Jerseyans tend to cheer for teams that play in New York or Pennsylvania.

Industries

New Jersey has a lot of jobs in the technology industry. Many people specialize in how computers run and making them run well. Others work with medicines and **biotechnology**.

The Jersey Devil

A strange creature is believed to live in the forests of southern New Jersey. It is known as the Jersey Devil. The Jersey Devil is said to have a horse's face on a dog's head. The creature is also believed to have bat-like wings, horns, hooved feet, and a tail.

New Jersey cranberries are harvested in bogs like this one. The farmers can wade through the water to inspect their crops.

Another important industry in New Jersey is agriculture. The Garden State grows many crops for the nation. These include fruits such as cranberries, peaches, and blueberries. Top vegetables grown there are eggplants, spinach, and tomatoes.

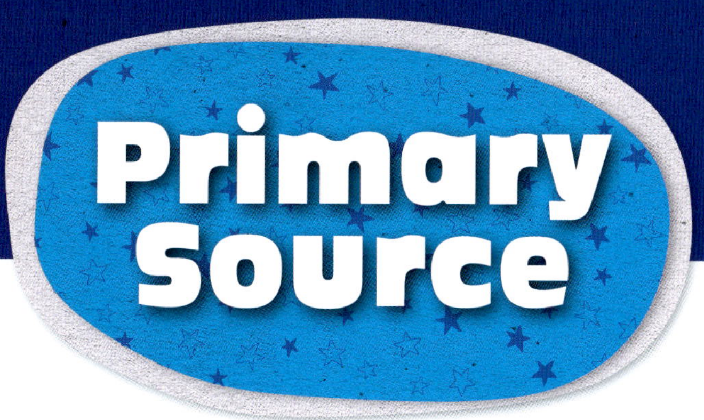

The Nanticoke and Lenape tribes describe the lives of their **ancestors**:

> [Our] ancestors were peace loving and given to hospitality. We lived in harmony with the natural world around us. . . . We honored the Creator . . . by respecting all life.

Source: "Our Ancient Way of Life." *Nanticoke and Lenape Confederation Learning Center and Museum*, 4 May 2010, nanticokelenapemuseum.org. Accessed 22 Oct 2023.

Comparing Texts

Think about the quote. Does it support the information in this chapter? Or does it give a different perspective? Explain how in a few sentences.

The Steel Pier is a part of the Atlantic City boardwalk. It is an amusement park that opened in 1898.

CHAPTER 3

Places in New Jersey

Trenton is New Jersey's capital city. It sits on the Delaware River in the center of the state. The city of Newark has the largest population in the state. Camden is another large city in southern New Jersey. Atlantic City is a big tourist spot. It sits on the Atlantic Ocean.

The Sandy Hook Lighthouse has stood since 1764.

Parks and Landmarks

New Jersey is known for the Jersey Shore. It covers 130 miles (209 km) of Atlantic coastline. Millions of people visit its sandy beaches every summer.

The Shore has many **boardwalks**. Ocean City, Wildwood, and Asbury Park are some of the most popular. The boardwalks have arcade games, rides, and food. The Shore also has

11 lighthouses. Sandy Hook is the oldest working lighthouse in the United States.

The Pinelands National Reserve is an important natural area in New Jersey. It covers about 1.1 million acres (445,000 ha) in southern New Jersey. This area includes land known as the Pine Barrens. This ecosystem has sandy soil and several bodies of water. It is also home to many rare plants and animals.

Bird Paradise

The Edwin B. Forsythe National Wildlife Refuge is an important area for many bird species. It covers around 48,000 acres (19,425 ha) in southern New Jersey. More than 360 different bird species have been seen there. Birds can be seen in the refuge year-round.

The Delaware Water Gap sits on the border between New Jersey and Pennsylvania.

The Delaware Water Gap is in the northwestern part of the state. It includes 40 miles (64 km) of river for exploring

The New Jersey State House is one of the oldest state capitol buildings in the country. It was built in 1792.

and fishing. The Appalachian Trail runs through part of this area. This trail covers almost 2,200 miles (3,540 km) of land. It stretches from Maine down to Georgia.

Washington Crossing is a historical landmark in both New Jersey and Pennsylvania. It was the site of an important battle during the American Revolutionary War (1775–1783).

A group of men reenact George Washington's famous Delaware River crossing. The man with the blue sash on his chest is playing General Washington.

On December 25, 1776, American army troops crossed the Delaware River. They landed nine miles (14 km) north of Trenton and surprised the enemy. A battle followed, which the Americans won. Today, people act out the crossing every December.

New Jersey is packed with many amazing sights. People can visit mountains and beaches. They can have fun at the many boardwalks at the Jersey Shore. And they can explore important historic sites. New Jersey has something to offer everyone.

Explore Online

Visit the website below. What new information did you learn about the Pinelands that wasn't in Chapter Three?

New Jersey Pinelands and Pine Barrens Overview

abdocorelibrary.com/discovering-new-jersey

State Map

KEY

Capital

Park

City or town

Point of interest

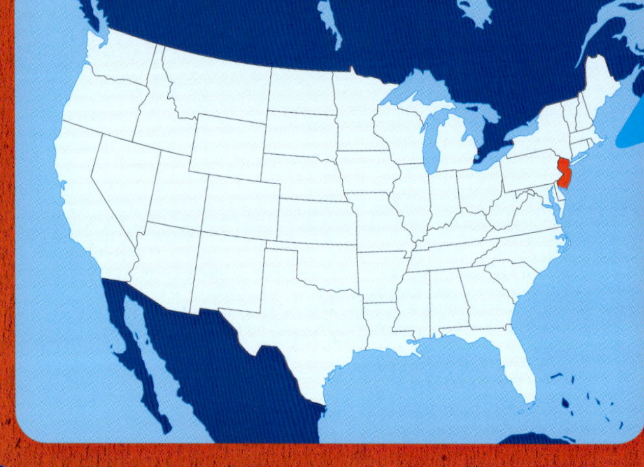

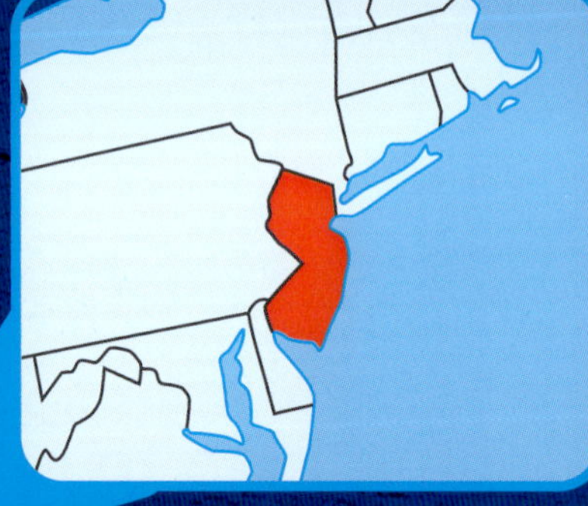

Ocean City

Delaware Water Gap

New Jersey: The Garden State
New York
Delaware Water Gap National Recreation Area
Hudson River
Paterson Great Falls National Historical Park
Delaware River
Newark
Jersey City
Sandy Hook Lighthouse
Washington Crossing State Park
Pennsylvania
Trenton
Asbury Park
Delaware River
JERSEY SHORE
Camden
Battleship New Jersey
New Jersey Pinelands National Reserve
Edwin B. Forsythe National Wildlife Refuge
Atlantic City
Delaware
Delaware Bay
Atlantic Ocean
N
W
E
S
Cape May

Glossary

ancestors
the people from whom a person is descended and who lived many generations ago

biotechnology
a science that uses living things such as cells and bacteria to make products

boardwalks
wooden walkways built along a beach

colonies
areas that are controlled by another country

duel
a fight between two people using weapons, often done to settle an argument

rivals
people who compete against one another to achieve the same thing

settled
moved into a new area

Online Resources

To learn more about New Jersey, visit our free resource websites below.

Visit **abdocorelibrary.com** or scan this QR code for free Common Core resources for teachers and students, including vetted activities, multimedia, and booklinks, for deeper subject comprehension.

Visit **abdobooklinks.com** or scan this QR code for free additional online weblinks for further learning. These links are routinely monitored and updated to provide the most current information available.

Learn More

Kavon, Kana. *The 50 States: Amazing Landscapes, Fascinating People, Wonderful Wildlife*. DK, 2021.

Murray, Julie. *New Jersey*. Abdo, 2020.

Index

About the Author

Janet Slingerland has authored more than two dozen nonfiction books on topics ranging from animals to Wi-Fi. She lives in New Jersey with her husband and three kids.